Maurice Pledger's

Bug World
sticker book

With over 300 reusable stickers!

A creepy-crawly sticker adventure

templar publishing

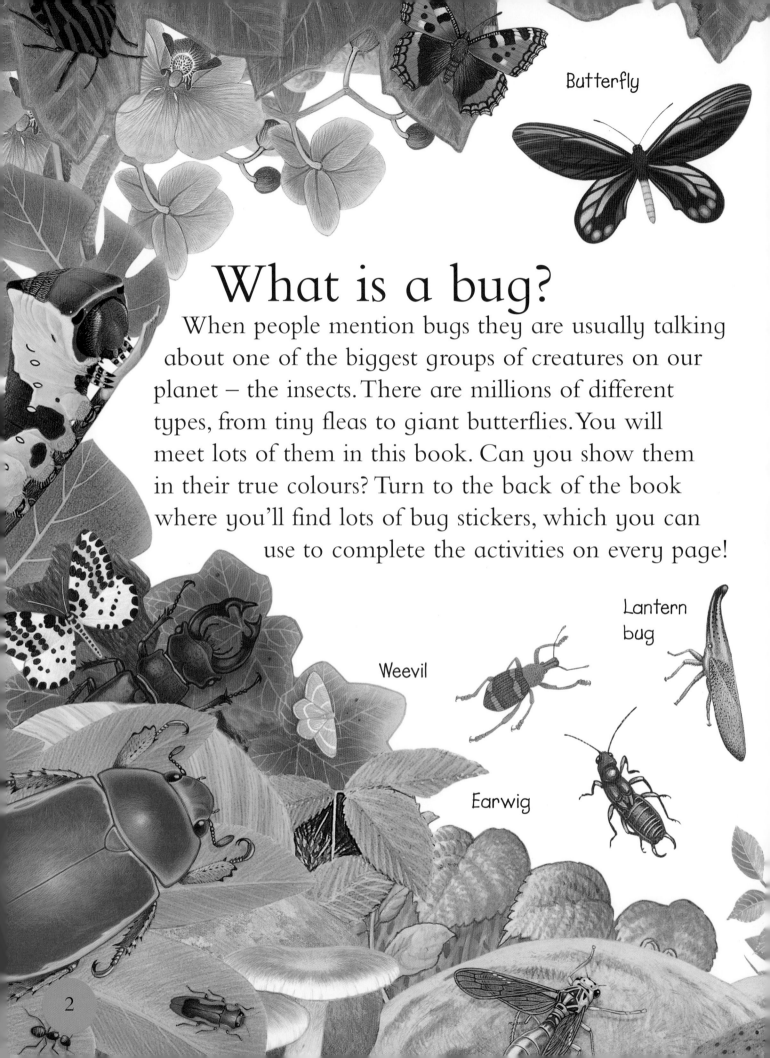

Butterfly

What is a bug?

When people mention bugs they are usually talking about one of the biggest groups of creatures on our planet – the insects. There are millions of different types, from tiny fleas to giant butterflies. You will meet lots of them in this book. Can you show them in their true colours? Turn to the back of the book where you'll find lots of bug stickers, which you can use to complete the activities on every page!

Lantern bug

Weevil

Earwig

Grasshopper

Flea

Beetle

Mantis

Fly

Ant

Stick insect

Moth

Bumblebee

3

Bug brothers

Not all creatures that you may call 'bugs' are from the insect family. An insect is a creature that has three body parts (head, middle and rear) plus six legs. Some bugs, like the centipede, have a lot more legs. Others, such as worms, have no legs at all. Find the stickers for the creepy-crawlies shown opposite before they scuttle, scurry or slither away!

Spider's web ►

Spiders belong to a group of creatures called arachnids. Spiders have eight legs and most produce silk, which they spin into webs to catch lunch, such as flies.

◄ Funnel web spider

This Australian spider lives in a burrow and weaves a funnel-shaped web at the entrance. Here it waits patiently for tasty bugs to get trapped in the web.

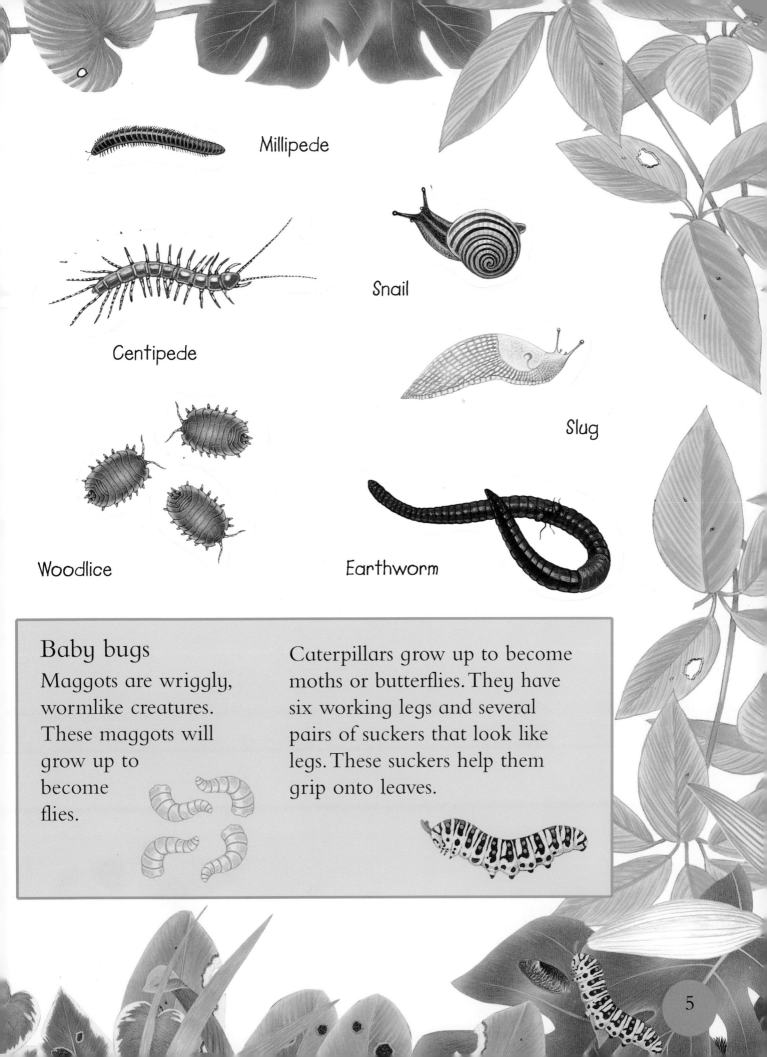

Millipede

Snail

Centipede

Slug

Woodlice

Earthworm

Baby bugs

Maggots are wriggly, wormlike creatures. These maggots will grow up to become flies.

Caterpillars grow up to become moths or butterflies. They have six working legs and several pairs of suckers that look like legs. These suckers help them grip onto leaves.

On the move

Bugs get around in all sorts of ways. Some, like the grasshoppers, can fly, jump and crawl, which helps them escape quickly from hunters, and also find food and mates. The fastest flyers are the dragonflies – with two pairs of wings, they can reach speeds of up to 60 kilometres per hour – that's almost as fast as a greyhound! Can you find the stickers for all of the acrobatic bugs shown here?

Treehopper

Tiger beetle

Lantern bug

Lichen cricket

Grasshopper

Caterpillar

Bee fly

Darter
dragonfly

Honeybee

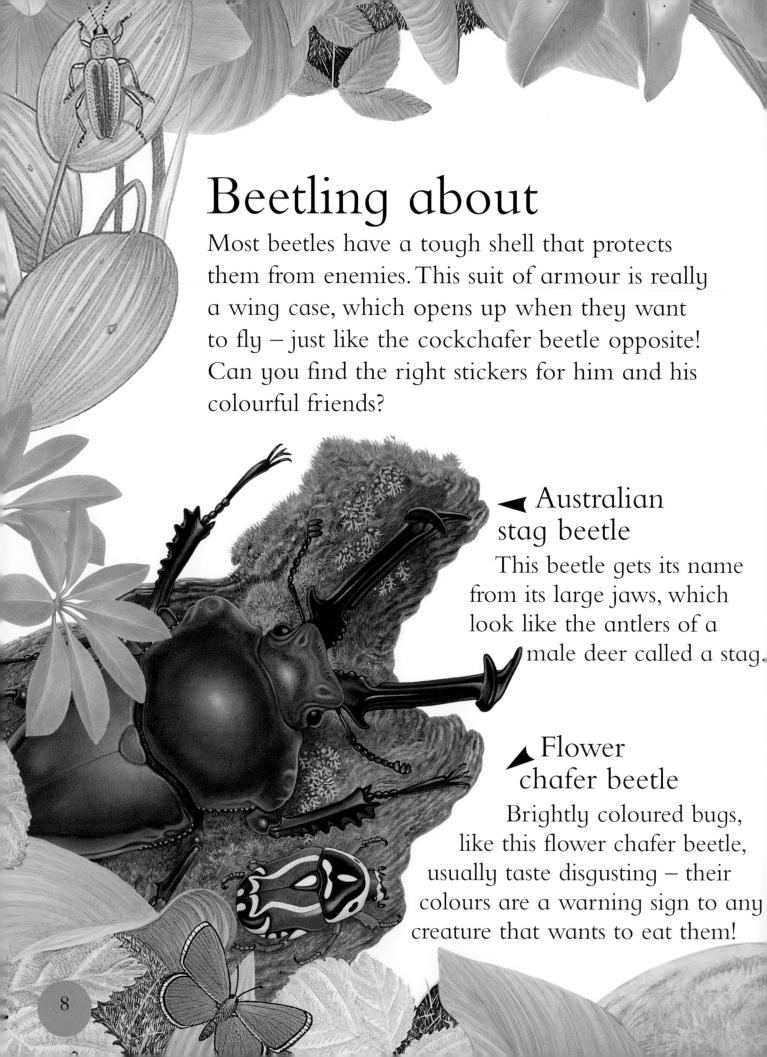

Beetling about

Most beetles have a tough shell that protects them from enemies. This suit of armour is really a wing case, which opens up when they want to fly – just like the cockchafer beetle opposite! Can you find the right stickers for him and his colourful friends?

◄ **Australian stag beetle**

This beetle gets its name from its large jaws, which look like the antlers of a male deer called a stag.

▲ **Flower chafer beetle**

Brightly coloured bugs, like this flower chafer beetle, usually taste disgusting – their colours are a warning sign to any creature that wants to eat them!

Cockchafer beetle

Bark weevil

Tortoise beetle

Golden scarab beetle

Hairy jewel beetle

Click beetle

Longhorn beetle

Jewel beetle

Darkling beetle

Colorado beetle

Seven-spot ladybird

Turn over to find a scene to use your stickers on.

Turn to the STICKER FUN section at the back of this book.

Can you find a nice home for your beetle buddies in this forest? Why not add some other bug friends too?

10

Who's hiding?

Most bugs want to stay hidden so they can sneakily catch other creatures to eat, while making sure they don't become someone else's lunch! The colours and patterns of some bugs help them blend in with the background.

Find the stickers for the bugs here and guess whether they like to hide among leaves, stems or branches…

◀Violin beetle
This beetle looks like a dark patch on a log.

▼Longhorn beetle
The stripes on this beetle make it blend in with the tree bark.

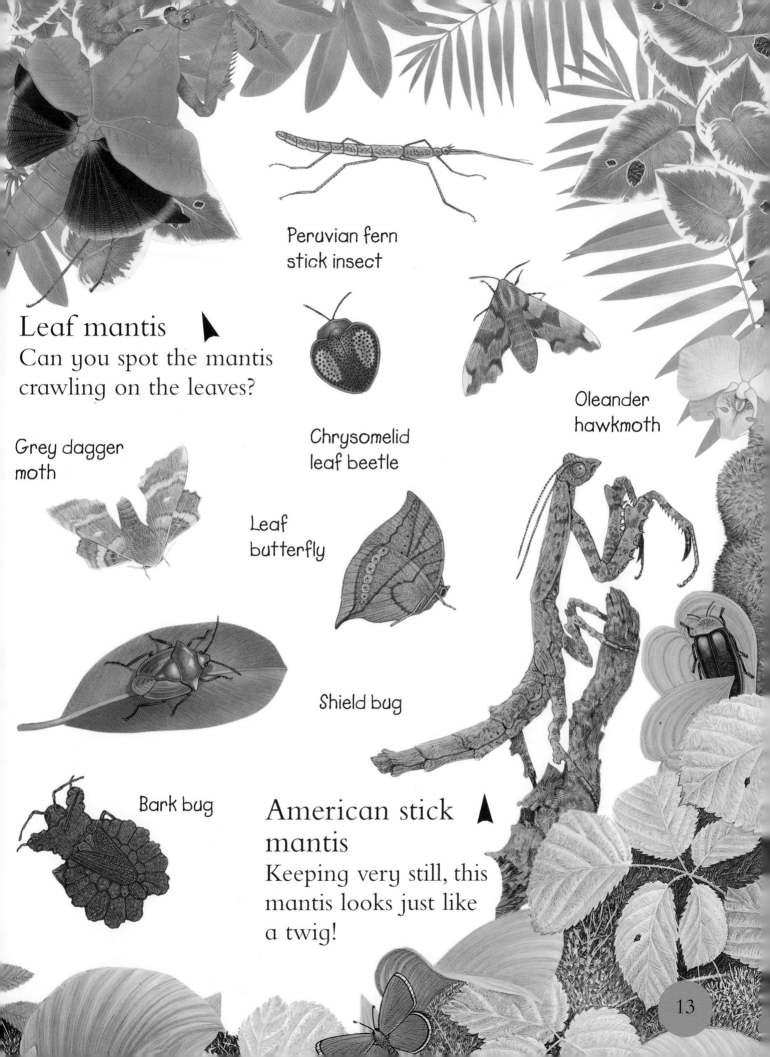

Peruvian fern stick insect

Leaf mantis ▶
Can you spot the mantis crawling on the leaves?

Oleander hawkmoth

Grey dagger moth

Chrysomelid leaf beetle

Leaf butterfly

Shield bug

Bark bug

American stick ▶ mantis
Keeping very still, this mantis looks just like a twig!

Strange shapes

Bugs come in all shapes and sizes. Some sneaky bugs will use their body shapes as a disguise to hide from hunters or to scare them away. Others use their bodies to attract a mate or store food. Can you match the strange shapes opposite with the correct creature stickers?

▼ Orchid mantis

This mantis has flaps on its body that look like petals. Some species can even change colour to match the flowers they are sitting on.

Peanut bug ▲

To other creatures in its jungle home, the peanut bug's head looks like a lizard's snout and the fake eyes on its wings make it look like a much larger animal.

Puss moth caterpillar

Thorn bugs

Treehopper

Giraffe-necked weevil

Leaf-legged bug

Honeypot ant

Lichen cricket

Lantern bug

Walking leaf bug
Can you see the leaf-shaped bug sitting on this plant?

15

Danger: bugs!

Why would a bug use bright colours instead of hiding away? Bright colours are often a warning to hunters that a bug tastes disgusting, or may sting or bite. Make the missing bugs here look more dangerous by finding their brightly coloured stickers.

◄ Click beetle
If its bright colours fail to warn off attackers, this beetle can launch itself into the air with a loud CLICK! to scare them away.

Garden tiger moth

Emperor moth

Polyphemus moth

When an enemy comes close, these four bugs spread their wings to reveal bright colours or spots that look like large eyes!

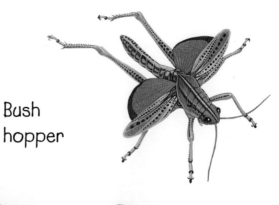

Bush hopper

These bugs are stripy. The honeybee and the wasp sting. The hoverfly does not, but is cleverly disguised to look like the other two.

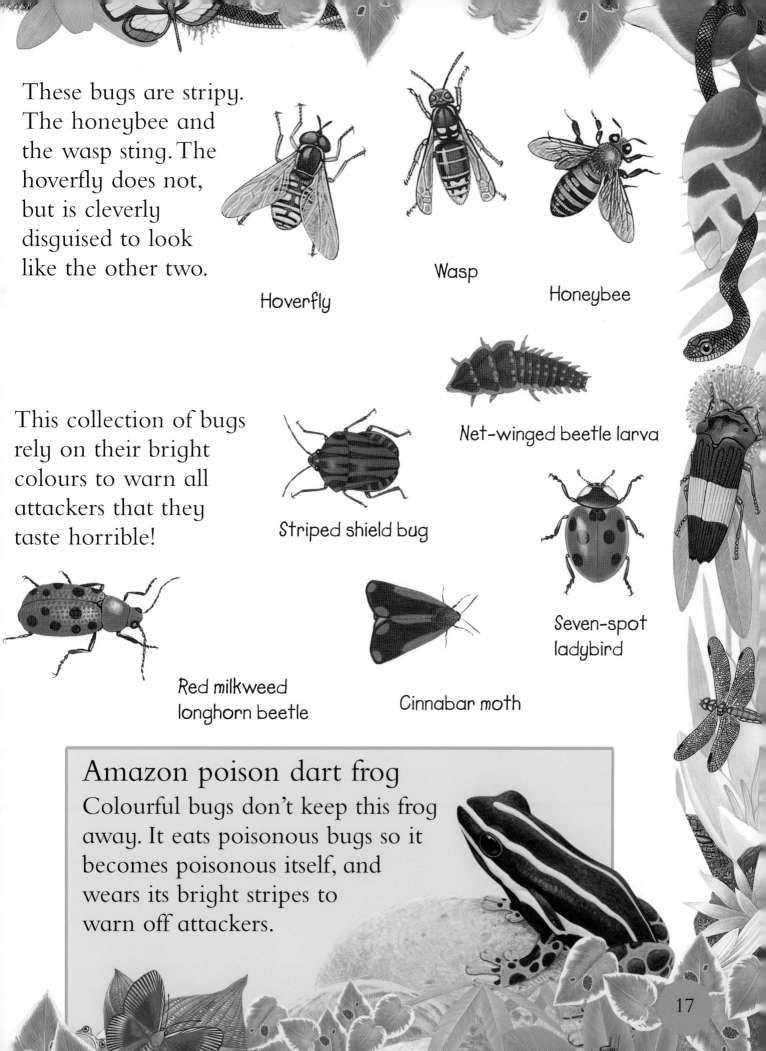

Hoverfly

Wasp

Honeybee

This collection of bugs rely on their bright colours to warn all attackers that they taste horrible!

Net-winged beetle larva

Striped shield bug

Seven-spot ladybird

Red milkweed longhorn beetle

Cinnabar moth

Amazon poison dart frog

Colourful bugs don't keep this frog away. It eats poisonous bugs so it becomes poisonous itself, and wears its bright stripes to warn off attackers.

Butterfly beauties

There are around 20,000 different types of butterfly, which can be found all over the world. The largest butterflies live in tropical rainforests and are much bigger than an adult's hand! How many different kinds of butterfly can you count on these pages?

Peacock butterfly

Richmond birdwing butterfly

Clouded sulphur butterfly

Glasswing butterfly

Purple hairstreak butterfly

Common blue
butterfly

Brimstone
butterfly

Oregon silverspot
butterfly

Common swallowtail
butterfly

Monarch butterfly

Queen Alexandra's
birdwing butterfly

Apollo jewel
butterfly

Small copper
butterfly

Fritillary butterfly

19

Magical moths

There are more than seven times as many different moths than there are butterflies. So how can you tell the difference? Most moths fly at night, while butterflies mainly fly during the day. Also, when they are at rest, butterflies will fold their wings up, whereas moths allows their wings to open out. How many different kinds of moth can you spot here?

Death's head hawkmoth

Leopard moth

American moon moth

Transparent burnet moth

Hummingbird hawkmoth

Red underwing moth

Chocolate tip
moth

Broad-bordered
bee hawkmoth

Indian
moon moth

Large emerald
moth

American
tiger moth

Bedstraw hawkmoth

Emperor moth

21

All change

You will have grown a lot since you
were a baby, but your body is still basically
the same. The only real difference is that now
you are bigger and stronger. A bug's life, on the
other hand, is not always quite so simple.
Many bugs go through incredible changes…

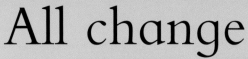

1. A butterfly begins life as an egg, laid on a leaf.

2. Each egg hatches out as a caterpillar, which feeds on the leaves.

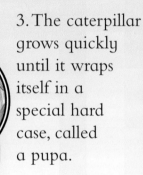

3. The caterpillar grows quickly until it wraps itself in a special hard case, called a pupa.

7. It spreads its wings to dry them in the sun before flying off.

4. Inside the pupa the caterpillar's body transforms…

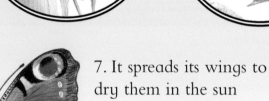

6. The creature that crawls out is an adult butterfly.

5. At last, the pupa splits open.

The nymph and the dragonfly

Dragonflies lay their eggs on plants in a pond or swamp. The bugs that hatch are called nymphs and they live underwater for up to four years, feeding on other small insects or fish. When a nymph is ready, it climbs up a plant stem to shed its skin, and out crawls an adult dragonfly.

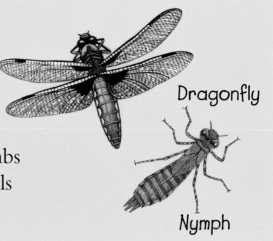

Dragonfly

Nymph

Can you find the stickers for each of these hungry caterpillars?

Monarch butterfly caterpillar

Spice bush swallowtail butterfly caterpillar

Cinnabar moth caterpillar

Privet hawkmoth caterpillar

Ghost moth caterpillar

Common swallowtail butterfly caterpillar

Berger's clouded yellow butterfly caterpillar

Poplar hawkmoth caterpillar

Gulf fritillary butterfly caterpillar

Eyed hawkmoth caterpillar

Garden tiger moth caterpillar

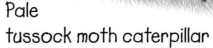

Pale tussock moth caterpillar

Turn over to find a scene to use your stickers on.

Can you add some colourful butterflies from the STICKER FUN sheets to this beautiful meadow scene?

24

Hive alive

Most bugs like to live alone but some prefer to build nests, or hives, that are home to thousands of relations. These bugs have to work together to look after the nest and gather food so they can all survive.

Bumblebee
While honeybees build nests in trees, bumblebees prefer abandoned burrows in the ground.

Queen bee
There is only one queen bee in a honeybee hive – she lays up to 2,000 eggs a day!

Wasp
Wasps make nests in tree hollows, bushes, inside the walls of houses or in holes in the ground.

Can you find the stickers for these busy creatures?

Inside a honeybee hive
Only one queen lives in the hive, along with a few male bees whose job it is to mate with her. The remaining bees in the hive are female workers that collect food, store honey and look after the young (called larvae).

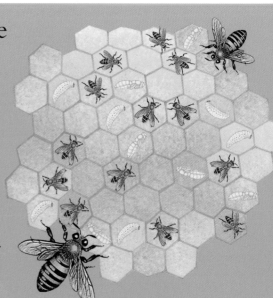

Jungle bugs

There are more bugs in a jungle than in any other habitat. Jungles stay warm and wet all year round – perfect for bugs to breed, feed and grow very big! How would you like to meet a beetle as big as your shoe or a moth as wide as both your outstretched hands? No? Then stay out of the jungle – find the jungle bug stickers instead!

Comet moth

◄ **Praying mantis**
This creature disguises itself as part of a plant, holding its spiked front legs in a praying position, ready to lunge forward to grab its lunch.

Goliath beetle

Hercules beetle

Tailed birdwing butterfly

Leaf-cutter ant

Cockroach

Morpho cacica butterfly

Golden scarab beetle

Giant metallic orchid bee

Jewelled frog beetle

Fantastic facts

Bugs may be small but they still get up to loads of amazing tricks! From the huge distances they travel to the way in which they look after their young, each one is keeping busy in its own clever way. Can you find the stickers for this bunch of incredible bugs?

The Robin's pincushion gall wasp lays its eggs inside a rose plant. The plant swells up around the young larvae and protects them. The swelling is called a gall.

Thousands of monarch butterflies go on a massive journey to lay their eggs – flying up to 2,900 kilometres!

Looking like pollen, the hairy jewel beetle can disguise itself inside a flower.

The carrion beetle's favourite food is the dead bodies of other creatures!

This hissing cockroach could survive for a week without its head!

The assassin bug dissolves the insides of its victim before sucking them up like soup!

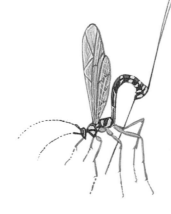

The ichneumon fly lays its eggs inside maggots. When the eggs hatch, the young eat the maggots from the inside out!

The darkling beetle releases a horrible smell to scare away its enemies.

Once the female glow-worm has mated, she turns out her light, lays her eggs and dies.

The tropical army ant travels in a group of several million ants – all produced by one queen!

Insect protection

Insects have a soft body that is protected by a tough outer case. However, if all else fails, they have a number of other sneaky ways to keep attackers at bay… Can you track down the stickers for each of the bugs opposite?

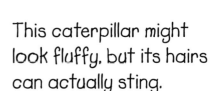

▼ **Prickly stick insect**
This stick insect, found in New Guinea and Australia, has a thorny armour that makes it difficult for a hungry creature to eat.

This caterpillar might look fluffy, but its hairs can actually sting.

The tiger beetle can run away quickly from any enemies.

These beetles all have a hard outer casing, which acts like a protective armour.

Atlas beetle

Dung beetle

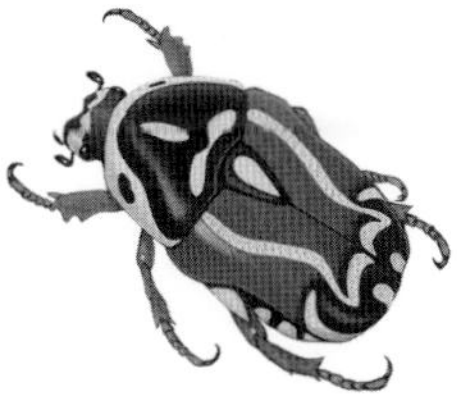

Flower chafer beetle

African tiger beetle

Golden scarab beetle

Longhorn beetle

If the ladybird's colours fail to frighten enemies, it oozes a smelly liquid from its leg joints.

This army ant has a nasty sting if anything gets too close.

This stinky bombardier beetle releases a smelly gas to keep all enemies away.

Record breakers

Can you imagine a person who could lift six large trucks or leap over the Great Pyramid of Giza in a single hop? Well, some record-breaking bugs can perform acts equally as impressive, considering their tiny size. Can you find the stickers for the super bugs shown here?

▼ Goliath beetle
This beetle is the heaviest in the world, weighing up to 100 grams – it's as heavy as a large apple, yet it can still fly.

▼ Hercules beetle
This South American beetle can lift more than 850 times its own body weight – similar to an adult human lifting six ten-tonne trucks.

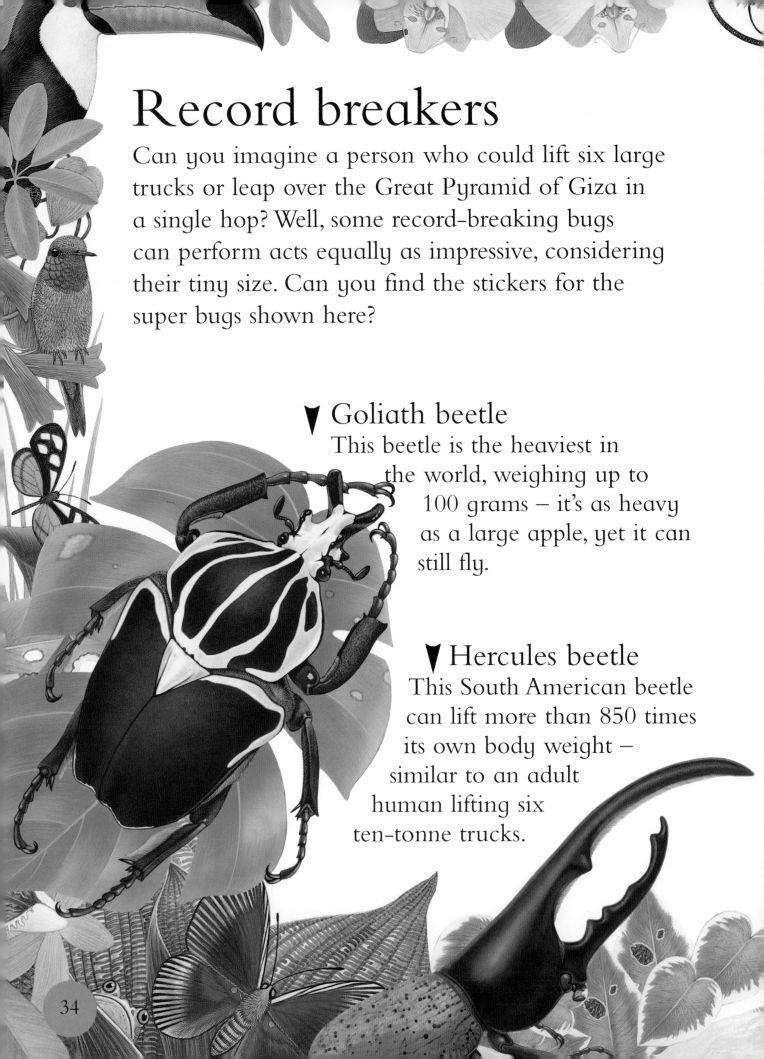

34

The world's smallest beetle, the feather-winged beetle, is so tiny that it can't be seen with the naked eye. Here it is next to a pin!

A flea can leap up to 30 centimetres, which is more than 130 times its own height – this would be like *you* leaping over the Great Pyramid.

This tropical atlas moth is the largest of all moths with a wingspan of 30 centimetres.

The male cicada is the loudest insect with a call that can be heard from almost a kilometre away!

The fastest species of tiger beetle can run up to 9 kilometres per hour.

The green darner dragonfly can reach speeds of over 30 kilometres per hour when flying from the southern United States to Canada to breed.

Titan beetle

Found in the Amazon rainforest, this is the world's largest beetle, at 20 centimetres long.

Bug builders

Bugs make great builders. Some wasps create delicate nests by chewing wood into a sticky pulp and moulding it into shape before it dries. Ants burrow deep underground to build their tunnelled homes. Can you find the stickers for the builder bugs opposite?

▼ Wasp
Some wasps make nests in tree stumps while others build nests out of mud.

Oak apple gall wasp with gall

▼ Dung beetle
This beetle rolls dung into a ball and lays its eggs inside. When the eggs hatch, the young grubs eat their way out of the ball.

Organ pipe mud
dauber wasp

Ants

Termite mound

Oak apple gall wasp

Termite

Inside a termite mound

Termite mounds are the
skyscrapers of the bug world.
Many are more than 7 metres
tall and a hundred years old.
Termites build their mounds out
of mud and spit. A large royal
chamber is built especially for
the queen termite to fit her
huge egg-laying body.

A bug for lunch

Bugs are a tasty snack for all sorts
of creatures, including reptiles, birds, other bugs
and even some plants! Turn to the STICKER FUN
pages to find a nice juicy bug for each
of these hungry critters.

▼ Bee-eater

The bee-eater uses its curved
beak to catch bees in flight.

▼ Giant anteater

The giant anteater rips open
ants' nests and termite mounds
before slurping up the
creatures inside.

Chameleon ◀

The chameleon
shoots out its long,
sticky tongue to
snatch bugs
off leaves.

Pitcher plant ▶

The pitcher plant traps bugs
inside and drowns them in
a liquid.

Water bugs

These bugs love water: flying above it, walking on it, swimming and diving in it or living underneath it. But they are not playing. They are hunting for food, laying their eggs and trying to avoid being eaten! How many different kinds of water bug can you find on these pages?

▼ Jewel-wing damselfly

Although the damselfly looks like a dragonfly, it is normally smaller and rests with its wings folded, while a dragonfly rests with its wings open.

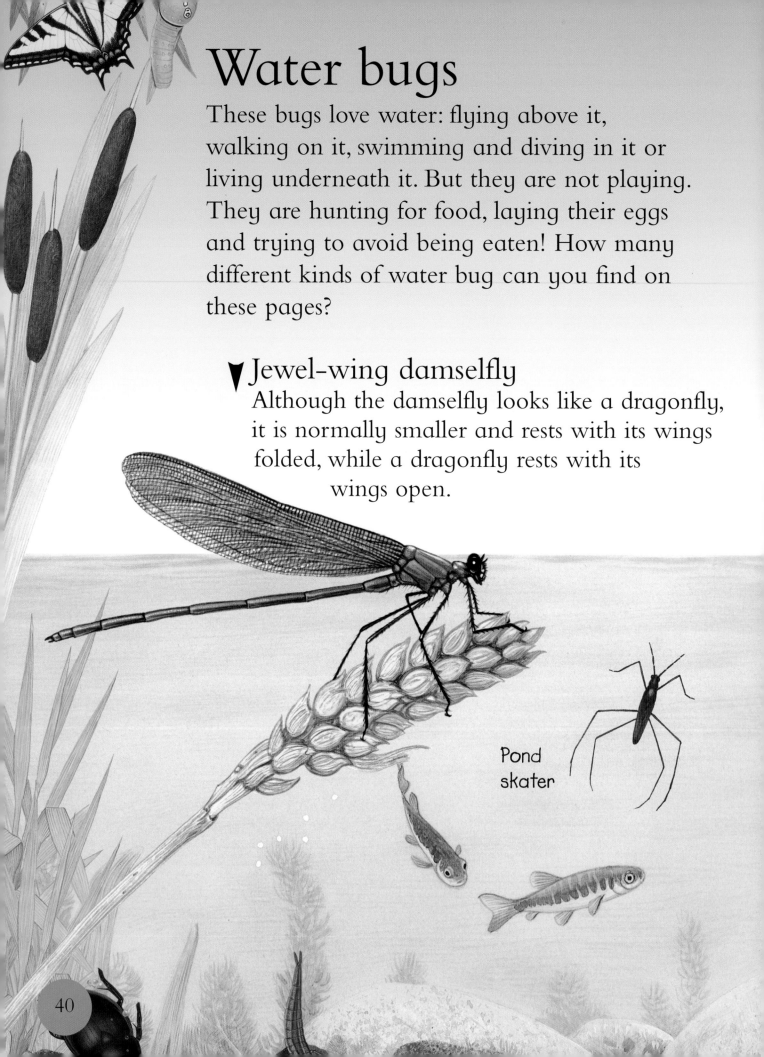

Pond skater

Common blue
damselfly

Crawling
mayfly

Emperor hawker
dragonfly

Darter dragonfly

Mosquito

Diving beetle

Water boatman

Dragonfly nymph

Turn over to find a scene to use your stickers on.

Turn to the STICKER FUN section and find some water bugs for the scene below – who lives in the water and who hovers above it?

43

In your garden

The best place for you to spot different kinds of bug is in your own garden or in the park. Find them feeding on the nectar of flowers, munching on leaves or hiding in the shade of a fallen log. But always remember that some bugs can bite or sting, so it's better to look and not touch.

It's time for STICKER FUN – can you find some creepy-crawlies for this garden home?

Can you find your favourite bugs of all from the STICKER FUN pages and add them to this forest?

How to use your stickers

Look for the page numbers on the sticker sheets at the back of this book to help you find the right stickers for the different bug activities. Peel each one carefully from its backing sheet and use it to fill in the shapes.

Whenever you see the words 'STICKER FUN', turn to the last section of the sticker sheets – here you will find lots of bug stickers to add to the extra picture scenes throughout the book.

Soon you will be able to name all of the creepy-crawlies. Then you'll be a bug expert!

Stickers for pages 2-3

Stickers for page 4-5

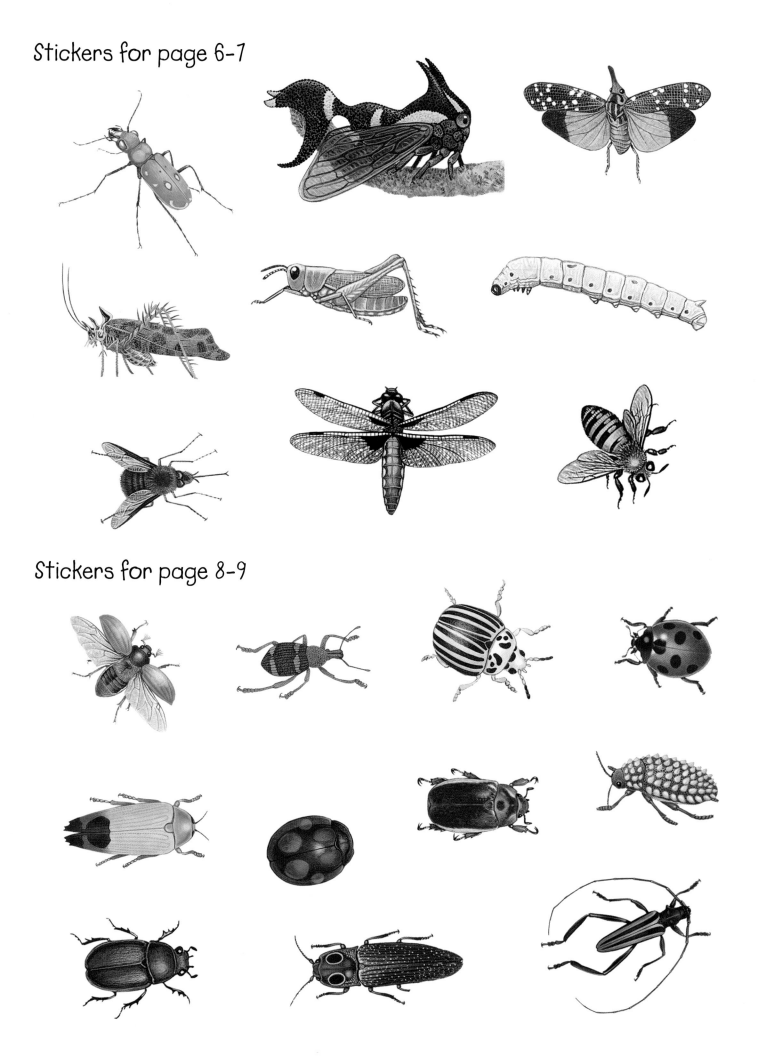

Stickers for page 6-7

Stickers for page 8-9

Stickers for pages 12-13

Stickers for pages 14-15

Stickers for pages 16-17

Stickers for pages 18-19

Stickers for pages 18-19 continued

Stickers for pages 20-21

Stickers for pages 20-21 continued

Stickers for pages 22-23

Stickers for pages 26-27

Stickers for pages 28–29

Stickers for pages 30–31

Stickers for pages 32-33

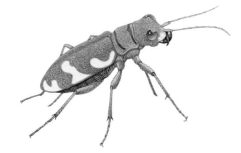

Stickers for pages 34-35

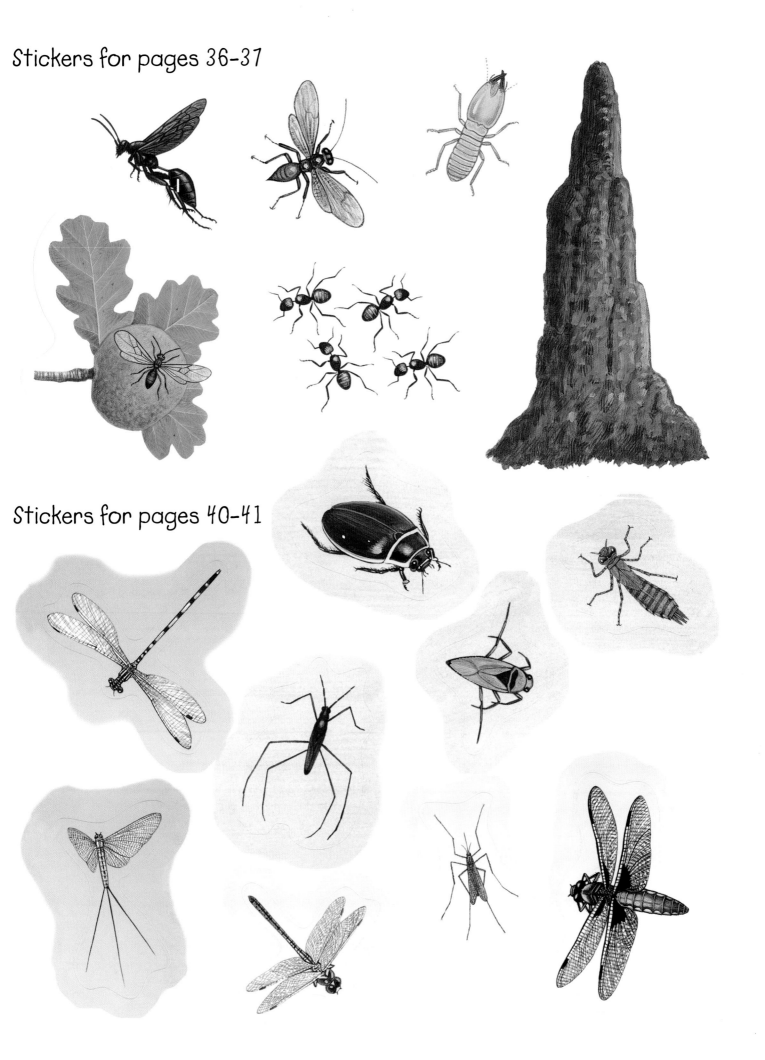

Stickers for pages 36-37

Stickers for pages 40-41

STICKER FUN: Use these extra stickers throughout the book to decorate your scenes.

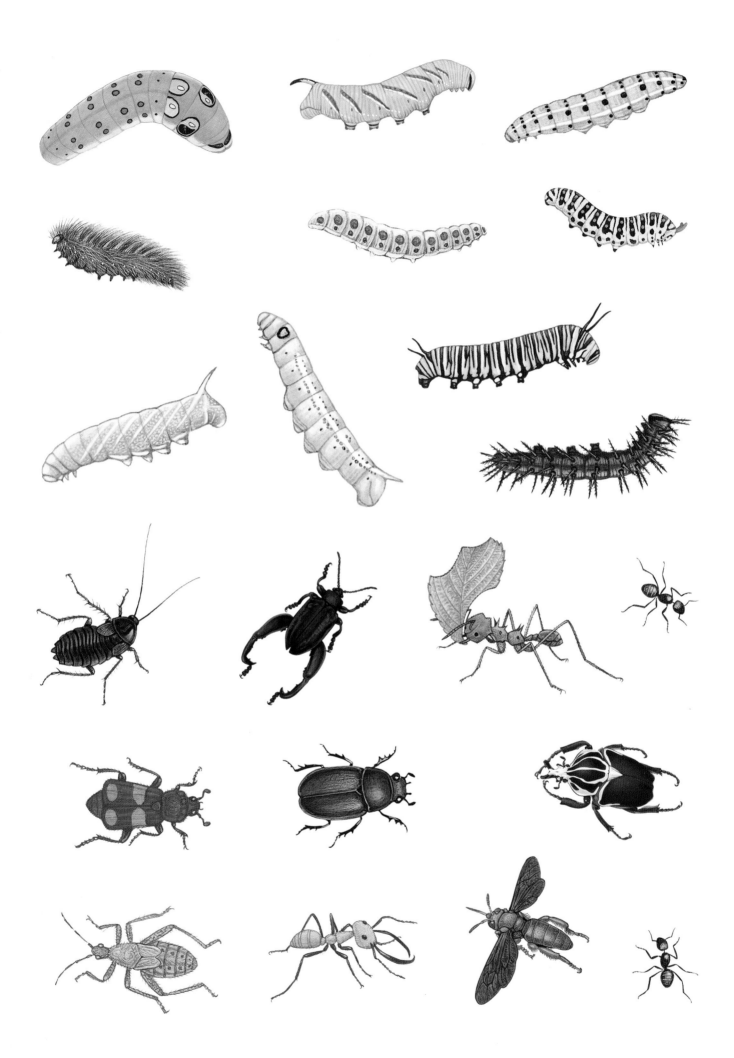